Happy Holidays!

Day of the Dead

by Betsy Rathburn

BELLWETHER MEDIA
MINNEAPOLIS, MN

Blastoff! Beginners are developed by literacy experts and educators to meet the needs of early readers. These engaging informational texts support young children as they begin reading about their world. Through simple language and high frequency words paired with crisp, colorful photos, Blastoff! Beginners launch young readers into the universe of independent reading.

Blastoff! Universe ★

Reading Level

Grade K

Grades 1-3

Grade 4

Sight Words in This Book 🔍

a	get	make	out	they
about	is	of	people	this
and	it	on	the	too
day	like	one	their	up
eat	look	other	these	

This edition first published in 2023 by Bellwether Media, Inc.

No part of this publication may be reproduced in whole or in part without written permission of the publisher. For information regarding permission, write to Bellwether Media, Inc., Attention: Permissions Department, 6012 Blue Circle Drive, Minnetonka, MN 55343.

Library of Congress Cataloging-in-Publication Data

Names: Rathburn, Betsy, author.
Title: Day of the Dead / by Betsy Rathburn.
Description: Minneapolis, MN : Bellwether Media, Inc., 2023. | Series: Blastoff! beginners. Happy holidays! | Includes bibliographical references and index. | Audience: Ages 4-7 | Audience: Grades K-1
Identifiers: LCCN 2022008855 (print) | LCCN 2022008856 (ebook) | ISBN 9781644877838 (library binding) | ISBN 9781648348501 (paperback) | ISBN 9781648348297 (ebook)
Subjects: LCSH: All Souls' Day--Juvenile literature. | Mexico--Social life and customs--Juvenile literature.
Classification: LCC GT4995.A4 R37 2023 (print) | LCC GT4995.A4 (ebook) | DDC 394.266--dc23/eng/20220223
LC record available at https://lccn.loc.gov/2022008855
LC ebook record available at https://lccn.loc.gov/2022008856

Editor: Christina Leaf   Designer: Laura Sowers

Printed in the United States of America, North Mankato, MN.

Table of Contents

It Is Day of the Dead!

Kids paint
their faces.
Today is
Day of the Dead!

A Happy Day

Day of the Dead
is on November 2.

It is a
Mexican holiday.
Other people
join, too.

People think about
lost loved ones.
It is a happy day!

Full of Color

People dress up.
They paint
their faces.
They look
like **skeletons**!

They make
altars.
These hold
candles and food.

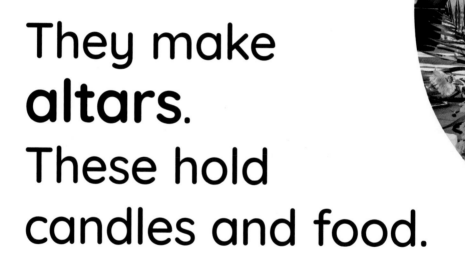

altar

They clean family **graves**. They put out flowers.

grave

People eat
sweet bread.

**sweet
bread**

They get
sugar skulls.
This day is
full of color!

sugar
skull

Day of the Dead Facts

Celebrating Day of the Dead

flowers

candles

sweet bread

Day of the Dead Activities

paint
faces

make
altars

clean
graves

Glossary

altars

tables where people leave things to honor the dead

graves

places that mark where the dead are buried

skeletons

bones that make up bodies

sugar skulls

colorful skeleton heads made of sugar

To Learn More

ON THE WEB

FACTSURFER

Factsurfer.com gives you a safe, fun way to find more information.

1. Go to www.factsurfer.com.

2. Enter "Day of the Dead" into the search box and click Q.

3. Select your book cover to see a list of related content.

Index